Climate Change

Robin Birch

Marshall Cavendish
Benchmark

New York

This edition first published in 2010 in the United States of America
by Marshall Cavendish Benchmark.

Marshall Cavendish Benchmark
99 White Plains Road
Tarrytown, NY 10591
www.marshallcavendish.us

All Internet sites were available and accurate when sent to press.

First published in 2009 by
MACMILLAN EDUCATION AUSTRALIA PTY LTD
15–19 Claremont Street, South Yarra 3141

Visit our website at www.macmillan.com.au or go directly to www.macmillanlibrary.com.au

Associated companies and representatives throughout the world.

Library of Congress Cataloging-in-Publication Data

Birch, Robin.
    Climate change / by Robin Birch.
        p. cm. – (Weather and climate)
    Summary: "Discusses how and why climates change over time, the climate changes that have occurred in the past,
    and the causes and effects of climate change today"–Provided by publisher.
    Includes bibliographical references and index.
    ISBN 978-0-7614-4473-2
    1. Climatic changes–Juvenile literature. I. Title.
    QC903.15.B57 2009
551.6–dc22

                                                                                    2009004982

Edited by Kylie Cockle
Text and cover design by Marta White
Page layout by Marta White
Photo research by Legend Images
Illustrations by Gaston Vanzet
Illustration on page 11 by James McKinnon

Printed in the United States

Acknowledgments
The author and the publisher are grateful to the following for permission to reproduce copyright material:

Front cover photograph: Aerial view of Disko Bay, Greenland, courtesy of Philippe Bourseiller/Getty Images
Photos courtesy of:
AAP Image/Dean Lewins, **29** (bottom); © Mepps/Dreamstime.com, **13** (top); © Rcmathiraj/Dreamstime.com, **21**; AFP/Getty
Images, **20**; J.W. Burkey/Getty Images, **30**; Grant Faint/Getty Images, **24**; Norbert Rosing/Getty Images, **23**; © Honda Motor
Co., Ltd, **29** (top); © Dan Eckert/iStockphoto, **27**; © Dawn Nichols/iStockphoto, **13** (bottom); NASA images by Jesse Allen and
Robert Simmon, based on MODIS data, **25**; NASA/Goddard Space Flight Center Scientific Visualization Studio, **22**; Photolibrary/
Jeff Friedman, **4**; Photolibrary/The Print Collector, **19**; © Dhoxax/Shutterstock, **5**; © Gail Johnson/Shutterstock, **10**; © Mary
Lane/Shutterstock, **8**; © Ales Liska/Shutterstock, **14**; © V.J. Matthew/Shutterstock, **28** (top); © Armin Rose/Shutterstock, **7**;
© Soundsnaps/Shutterstock, **26**; © vias2000/Shutterstock, **28** (bottom); SOHO (ESA & NASA), **15**; U.S. Geological Survey
Photograph taken on June 12, 1991, by Richard P. Hoblitt, **18**.

Contents

Glossary Words

When a word is printed in **bold**, you can look up its meaning in the Glossary on page 31.

Weather and Climate

What is the weather like today? Is it hot, cold, wet, dry, windy, or calm? Is it icy or snowy? Is there a storm on the way? We are all interested in the weather because it makes a difference in how we feel, what we wear, and what we can do.

The weather takes place in the air, and we notice it because air is all around us.

Climate

The word *climate* describes the usual weather of a particular place. If a place usually has cold weather, then we say that place has a cold climate. If a place usually has hot weather, we say it has a hot climate.

Farmers need to know about the weather so they can best look after their crops and animals.

Climate Change

Earth's climate changes over time. There have been cold periods and warm periods. If the weather is different from usual for many years, we say the climate has changed.

Climates can become hotter, colder, wetter, drier, and more or less windy. Huge changes in climate usually mean that the plants and animals of an area are replaced by different ones. Climate change can also make the **sea level** rise or fall.

Climates change because of changes in:

- the **atmosphere**
- ocean currents
- the shape of the land
- the Sun's **radiation**

Many scientists believe that some of the climate change of recent times has been caused by people.

In the past, most of Earth had a warm and humid climate and was covered by lush tropical forests like this.

Past Climates

Earth's climate has changed many times since Earth was formed 4,600 million years ago. When Earth formed, it did not have an atmosphere, so there was no climate.

Timeline of Past Climate Change

- By 3,500 million years ago, Earth had an atmosphere and oceans, but we do not know what the climate was like then.

- Earth became very cold and icy 2,700 million years ago. It warmed up and then became cold again 850 million years ago. These cold periods are known as "ice ages."

- By 400 million years ago, the climate became suitable for plants and animals to live on land and in the oceans. Since then, Earth has twice become very cold again.

Weather Report

Earth's **continents** have moved around over time, joining together and breaking apart, until becoming today's continents. They are still moving slowly.

Timeline of Climate Change

Earth formed — 4,600 mya
Atmosphere and oceans formed — 3,500 mya
Ice age — 2,700 mya
Ice age — 850 mya
Plants and animals — 400 mya
Today

(mya = million years ago)

During the ice ages,
parts of Earth would have
looked similar to this.

The Age of the Dinosaurs

Dinosaurs lived on Earth from 245 million years ago to 65 million years ago.
During this time, most of Earth had a warm climate. The climate was also humid,
which means there was moisture in the air and high levels of rainfall.

The warmth and high levels of rainfall of this time meant that many plants could
grow. There were trees, shrubs, ferns, and mosses. There was no grass.

In the time of the dinosaurs, the North and South **Poles** were in different places
from where they are now. These areas were cooler than other places on Earth,
and they had long periods of winter darkness. The polar areas had **frosts**,
but were not covered in ice and snow as polar areas are today.

The Ice Ages

An ice age is a period of time when it gets very cold over much of Earth. Large parts of Earth become covered with **ice sheets**, **glaciers**, and snow. Other parts become cool and dry.

Earth has had four major ice ages. The fourth one is still in progress. This ice age is often called the Great Ice Age. It began about 3 million years ago.

During an ice age, large amounts of water become ice. This means there is less water available for rainfall and the oceans. As a result, there is less rain, the land becomes drier, and sea levels drop.

The Four Major Ice Ages

Ice Age	Millions of Years Ago
first	2,700 to 2,300
second	850 to 630
third	350 to 260
fourth	3 to today

Ice sheets covered large areas of land during all four ice ages.

The Great Ice Age

The Great Ice Age started about 3 million years ago and is still continuing. It is an ice age that has had warm and cold periods. Earth is now in one of the warm periods.

The most recent cold period ended 10,000 years ago. In this cold period, ice sheets and snow covered the northern parts of Europe, Asia, and North America. Huge glaciers, at times several thousand feet thick, spread across these areas. There were also glaciers on the mountains on the other continents.

The sea level was lower in the last cold period. This meant there was more land around the continents. People who lived at this time could walk across areas that are now covered by sea.

Weather Report

Up to 10,000 years ago, there were glaciers on mountains on all the continents. Today, most of the world's glaciers are in New Zealand, Antarctica, Europe, and North America.

Ice covered much of the Earth's surface more than 10,000 years ago during the last ice age.

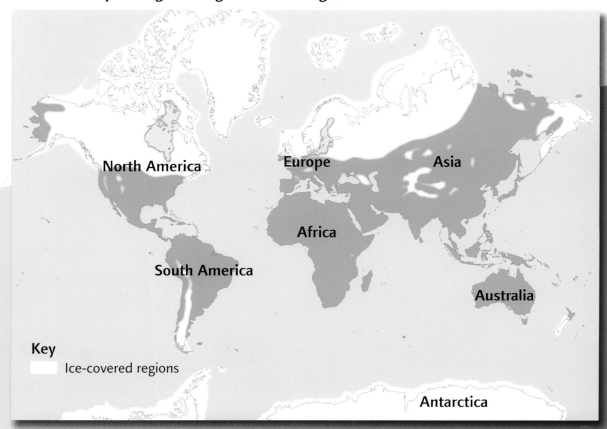

North America

Europe

Asia

Africa

South America

Australia

Key

Ice-covered regions

Antarctica

Early Humans

The first humans lived about 2.4 million years ago in what is now known as Africa, in the eastern region around present-day Ethiopia and Kenya. This was a time when Earth entered the Great Ice Age, and climates were becoming drier.

Humans started spreading out about 2 million years ago. They spread out through Europe, Asia, and the rest of Africa. Scientists think they may have **migrated** because of changes in the climate of the **Sahara** area. This area has changed from wet grasslands to dry **desert** several times. Dry weather may have forced the people to move away.

Early humans are often called cavemen. This is a name commonly given to the people who lived in the northern parts of the world that were very cold and icy during the Great Ice Age. These people hunted animals for food and clothing.

Weather Report

As Africa entered the Great Ice Age it became drier, and many of the forests died out and were replaced by grasslands. The first humans lived in these grassland areas.

The Sahara is a desert today, but may have looked like this in the past.

Humans and Large Animals

Cool climates led to the development of large animals. Their large bodies were better at keeping in the heat. In northern parts of the world there were woolly mammoths, cave lions, and giant beavers. In Australia there were huge **diprotodons** and giant kangaroos.

These large animals were hunted by early humans in different parts of the world, until about 10,000 years ago. This is when the most recent cold period of the Great Ice Age ended. Most of the world's large animals became **extinct** at this time.

We do not know whether the giant animals became extinct because of the change in climate or for other reasons. They could have been overhunted by humans.

This giant kangaroo had teeth that suggest it was a meat-eater.

Climates Today

At present, Earth has nine different climate zones. Places that have similar climates are in the same climate zone. Plants and animals that live in these different zones are suited to live in these **environments**.

Wet and Dry Climates

Name of Zone	Features	Plants
tropical	warm or hot temperatures high humidity high rainfall	rain forests
subtropical	warm or hot temperatures high rainfall wet and dry seasons	grasslands woodlands
arid	very dry hot deserts cold deserts	tough, low-growing plants
semiarid	low rainfall dry	grasslands

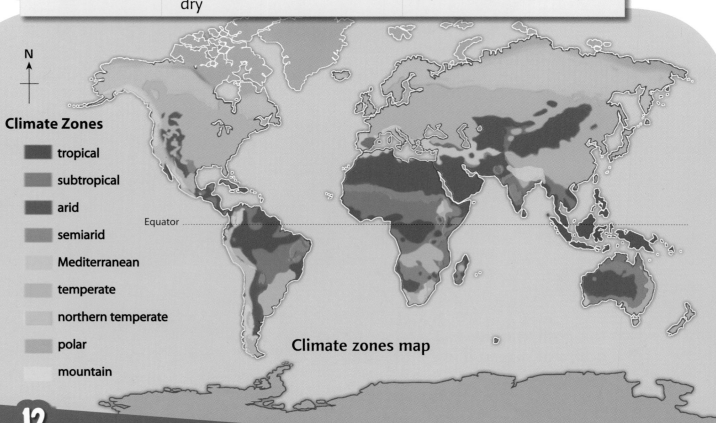

N

Climate Zones

- tropical
- subtropical
- arid
- semiarid
- Mediterranean
- temperate
- northern temperate
- polar
- mountain

Equator

Climate zones map

Deciduous trees grow in temperate zones.

Hot and Cold Seasons

The Mediterranean zone has cool, wet winters and very hot, dry summers. The shrubs and trees that grow here can survive the dry summers.

The temperate zone has four distinct seasons: spring, summer, fall, and winter. These areas have good rainfall, which is higher in summer. Areas in the temperate zone are known for their **deciduous** trees with colorful fall leaves.

Cold Climates

The northern temperate zone is only found in the northern **hemisphere**. It has short, cool summers and long, cold winters. **Forests** of **conifers** grow in these zones.

The polar zone surrounds Earth's North and South Poles. It is very cold and dry, and ice and snow cover much of the land all year round.

The mountain zone is found at the tops of very high mountains on various parts of Earth. The air is very thin, and there is snow and ice. Only tough, low-growing plants can survive in this environment.

The climate is very severe in the mountain zone.

13

Climate Change

Climates have changed since Earth was formed. These changes in the climates have affected all living things.

Animals and Plants

Animals and plants are suited to the place they live. They have features that help them to survive. For example, cold-weather animals have thick hair or fur. If the weather becomes very different for a long period of time, plants and animals can often no longer live in the same area. They may die out, or they may move to other places.

People

Throughout history, people have also relied on the weather to survive. If the weather changed, they would not always have been able to live in the same place. They may not have been able to grow their crops, for example. People think that some **civilizations** may have disappeared because of climate change.

Since Earth formed, there have been five **mass extinctions** of plants and animals. These may have been caused by changing climate.

The ancient Mayan civilization may have disappeared because of a very long period of drought.

Natural Causes of Climate Change

There are several reasons why climates have changed over time:

- Since Earth formed 4,600 million years ago, the Sun has been slowly getting brighter and hotter. This has given Earth more light and warmth.

- Earth circles the Sun in a path called an orbit. The orbit slowly changes from a circle to an oval every 100,000 years. When Earth is closer to the Sun, it gets more heat and light.

- The position of Earth's North and South Poles has changed over time. This causes climate change because the poles have long, dark winters that last for weeks or months.

Weather Report

The weather is affected by dark spots on the Sun, known as sunspots. These increase and decrease in number over an eleven-year period, which brings about changes in the Sun's radiation. If the Sun has more sunspots, it is hotter and brighter than usual.

These dark spots on the Sun are huge sunspots.

Moving Continents

The outer layer of the Earth is called the crust. The crust is broken up into several different pieces called plates. Earth's lands (continents and islands) are on these plates. The plates, and the land on them, move slowly over time. This process is known as continental drift.

Continental drift has changed climates. For example, Australia, New Guinea, South America, Africa, Arabia, India, and New Zealand all used to be joined to Antarctica, and formed one huge land known as Gondwana. When these lands moved apart, deep ocean currents began circulating around Antarctica. This caused Antarctica to cool down, and ice sheets began to form on it about 40 million years ago.

Gondwana was a super-continent that finished breaking apart 45 million years ago.

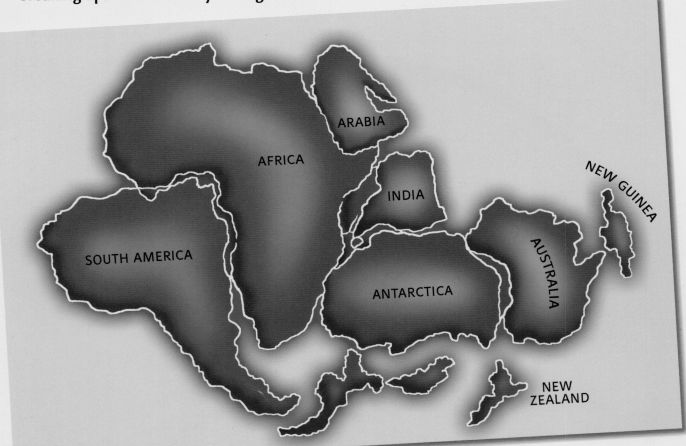

Ocean Currents

Oceans have rivers of water flowing in them called ocean currents. All of these currents move warm and cold water around Earth. They affect the weather because the oceans warm or cool the air above them, and that air is blown over land by winds. When ocean currents change, it brings about changes in climate.

Ocean currents on the surface are blown along by winds. Changes in the winds bring changes to the currents. But changes to the currents also bring changes to the winds, by warming or cooling air, so the air and water systems affect each other closely. Even small changes to ocean circulation can cause changes to the climate.

Ocean currents form an ocean conveyor belt. Surface water sinks and then moves along very slowly deep down. Some water takes 1,600 years to circulate once through the oceans.

Water in the oceans flows in currents.

warm current
cold current

Meteorites, Comets, and Volcanoes

In the past, when **meteorites** and **comets** have crashed into Earth, they have thrown up huge amounts of dust into the atmosphere. This dust partly blocked out the Sun's light and heat, and caused the atmosphere to cool down.

Volcanoes have also caused cooling by filling the atmosphere with dust and ash. For example, the eruption of Mount Pinatubo in the Philippines in 1991 affected the weather for years. Huge eruptions occur only a few times every hundred million years, but can change the climate for millions of years and cause mass extinctions.

Some scientists have suggested that a meteorite or comet may have caused the extinction of many plants and animals at the time the dinosaurs died out, which was about 65 million years ago.

The eruption plume of gases and ash from Mount Pinatubo reached 21 mi high (34 kilometers) and was more than 249 mi wide (400 km).

This scene shows a frost fair on
the frozen Thames River in London, 1683.
The winters were particularly cold in the Little Ice Age.

Unusual Weather

Sometimes the weather has changed for a while, and then returned to normal afterward. These changes are not considered true climate change.

The Little Ice Age

From about 1550 to 1850, much of the world experienced very cold winters. This period has been called the Little Ice Age. It may have been caused by volcanic ash in the atmosphere and the Sun giving off less heat at that time.

El Niño

El Niño is a weather pattern that takes place every few years. It causes changes to ocean currents. The usually cold water in the eastern Pacific Ocean switches with the warm water in the western part of the Pacific Ocean. The winds also swap direction. El Niño brings drought in Australia and Southeast Asia. The Asian **monsoon** becomes weaker. Heavy rain falls in western North and South America.

Weather Report

El Niño means "the little boy" in Spanish.

Global Warming

Today, many scientists, governments, and everyday people are talking about global warming. They are talking about the discovery that Earth's atmosphere and oceans have become a little warmer. Many scientists have predicted that the atmosphere and oceans will continue to become warmer in the future. These scientists believe that this will affect the weather, the oceans, and the land, and that these changes may even be happening already.

Scientists have discovered that the temperature of the atmosphere near Earth's surface has increased by 1.4 degrees Fahrenheit (0.8 degrees Celsius) in the one hundred years up to 2005. This is only a very small change, but scientists believe the changes could be greater in the future.

These scientists are at a meeting of governments to discuss climate change.

More places may become warm and humid if Earth's climate warms up.

Possible Problems

Many scientists believe that global warming brings changes in the weather by causing:

- more storms
- wetter weather in some areas
- drier weather in others

The changes in the weather could bring about changes in **vegetation** to many places.

The ice sheets and glaciers at the North and South Poles are already melting and breaking away. If this continues there will be a lot less ice and snow at the poles. Global warming may bring about a rise in sea levels, so low-lying coastal areas become swamped with seawater. This would mean that people who live in low-lying coastal areas would lose their homes and land.

Weather Report

The changes to the weather may bring trouble for farmers, such as crop failure and diseases in plants and animals. There could be financial problems for many people.

Melting Polar Ice

Many people are concerned about the melting of the ice at the North and South Poles, and that the sea levels are rising.

Polar Ice

Polar ice is the name of the ice around the North and South Poles. The area around the North Pole is known as the Arctic. The Arctic Ocean lies over the North Pole itself, and there is land around it, such as Greenland. There is thick ice on the Arctic Ocean and on Greenland. Thick ice that floats on the sea is called pack ice.

Antarctica is a continent that lies over the South Pole. It has a thick ice sheet over most of it and **ice shelves** that extend out over the sea.

Weather Report

The Wilkins Ice Shelf is an ice shelf in the Antarctic. In March 2008, a huge part of it broke away. Scientists think it may have broken up because the temperatures in the area have been rising.

The Arctic pack ice after the summer of 1979.

The Arctic pack ice after the summer of 2003. Note the reduction over twenty-four years.

Melting Ice

Satellite photographs have shown that pack ice on the Arctic Ocean now covers a smaller area than before. It is also not as thick as it was. By 2013, scientists think there may be no summer ice on the Arctic Ocean. The ice sheet on Greenland has also become smaller in the summer than it used to be.

The ice shelves around Antarctica also cover a smaller area than they did a few years ago.

Animals

When pack ice melts it affects the animals who live on it, such as polar bears, seals, and walruses, because the area gets smaller. These animals also rely on the pack ice for food, because **microscopic** plants grow in the water under the pack ice. The plants provide food for fish and other small water animals that are eaten by the animals who live on the ice.

Weather Report

In the summer, pack ice on the Arctic Ocean has broken up so much that ships can now cross from the Atlantic Ocean to the Pacific Ocean, in a path known as the Northwest Passage.

Walruses eat small water animals, such as shrimp, crabs, and clams.

Sea Levels

Earth's sea levels barely changed from 3,000 years ago to the year 1800. Scientists have discovered that since 1870, sea levels have risen about 0.07 inches (1.7 millimeters) per year, and that they are rising at a faster rate all the time.

Ice is not as heavy as water. Also, when ice floats, most of it stays underwater. When ice that floats on the sea melts, it does not make any difference to the sea level.

Seawater Temperature

When white ice and snow cover the sea, they reflect the Sun's heat, which keeps the water underneath cold. If this ice and snow melt, the sea becomes exposed to the Sun, and it wams up. As it warms, more ice melts, so the water warms up even more. When water warms up it expands, so the sea level becomes higher. This has been the main cause of rising sea levels so far.

This floating ice is called an iceberg. Most of it is underwater.

Ice Sheet Breakup

The ice sheet that covers Greenland is up to 1.9 mi (3 km) thick at its thickest point. It is a clear blue-green color in the winter. The temperature is −4 to −22°F (−20 to −30°C). The ice sheet that covers Antarctica is much larger and colder. It is around 1.9 mi (3 km) thick and has a temperature of −35°F (−37°C).

On land, when pieces of ice break off ice sheets and glaciers and fall into the sea, they make the sea level rise a small amount. Antarctica is too cold for the ice sheet on land to melt or break, but the ice sheet on Greenland has broken up a little.

In 2007, scientists studied information from satellites and detected lakes and rivers underneath the Antarctic ice sheet. They are concerned that this may cause the ice sheet to break up.

The Wilkins Ice Shelf on February 28, 2008.

The Wilkins Ice Shelf on March 17, 2008. The arrow shows where the ice shelf has broken away and fallen into the sea.

The Greenhouse Effect

The atmosphere forms an envelope around Earth. Many heat and light **rays** from the Sun pass through the atmosphere and reach the ground. The atmosphere stops about 70 percent of these rays from bouncing away from Earth and going out into space. This process is called the greenhouse effect.

The main **gases** in the atmosphere are oxygen, nitrogen, and argon. These gases have little effect on the Sun's rays. The gases that stop rays from escaping into space are water **vapor**, carbon dioxide, and ozone. When there are more of these gases in the atmosphere, Earth becomes warmer.

The greenhouse effect gets its name from greenhouses used to house plants.

Cars produce carbon dioxide in their exhaust.

More Carbon Dioxide

Scientists have discovered there is more carbon dioxide in the atmosphere today than there used to be. Many scientists believe this may be the reason why the temperature of the atmosphere has increased.

The increase in the greenhouse effect is known as the enhanced greenhouse effect. The enhanced greenhouse effect may be caused by people, or by natural events such as volcano eruptions and other things that have caused climate change in the past.

Weather Report

Some volcanoes release great amounts of carbon dioxide gas into the atmosphere. This leads to a warmer atmosphere.

People and Climate

Burning coal to make electricity releases carbon dioxide into the atmosphere.

People contribute to climate change by releasing carbon dioxide into the atmosphere and by the way that they use the land.

Carbon Dioxide

Carbon dioxide is released when fuels such as wood, coal, gas, and oil are burned. Coal, gas, and oil are known as fossil fuels. Carbon dioxide is also released from factories, when coal is burned to make electricity, and from car motors. A huge increase in the number of people, cars, and factories in recent years means there has been much more carbon dioxide produced.

Land Use

In many places, farmers have cut down trees in order to clear more land to grow crops or raise livestock. When the land is cleared, the soil is easily washed or blown away. This has led to the drying out of the soil and vegetation dying, so the areas have become more desertlike.

As the world's population grows, more land will need to be cleared to grow food.

What We Can Do

Many people are trying to find ways to stop or slow down the climate change that has been happening in recent years.

- We can make less carbon dioxide. **Solar power** and wind power are two ways of making electricity without burning fossil fuels. Solar hot water and better housing design cut down on power use. If we drive cars that don't use fossil fuels and change the way factories operate, we can also cut down on the amount of carbon dioxide released into the atmosphere.

- We can use the land better. We can plant trees and shrubs that will serve as **windbreaks**, keep soil in place, and hold moisture in the soil. Mulch and compost on soil also keep moisture in, and make it easier to grow crops. People have even made dry land usable by doing these things.

- We can make agreements with other countries. The Kyoto Protocol is an example of an agreement that was made between countries about their carbon dioxide release. It was made in Kyoto, Japan, in 1997. Many countries are participating in the agreement, which means that they are making a **commitment** to produce less carbon dioxide.

This car runs on hydogen fuel cells and does not produce carbon dioxide emissions.

This house is designed to stay cool in a hot climate, and to save the electricity usually used for air conditioning.

29

Weather Wonders

The concentration of carbon dioxide in the atmosphere has increased by about 35 percent since the year 1800, when there was an increase in industry in many countries.

Antarctica is colder than the Arctic. Away from the coast, temperatures in Antarctica reach between −112 and −130°F (−80 and −90°C) in the winter.

A large piece of ice that floats in seawater is called an iceberg. Only one tenth of an iceberg shows above water.

The Kyoto Protocol is part of the United Nations Framework Convention on Climate Change. This is a treaty, and it expires in 2012.

Glossary

atmosphere layer of air around Earth

civilizations highly developed human societies

comet bright space object with a cloudy tail that orbits the Sun

commitment promise

conifers trees with needlelike leaves and cones that hold seeds

continents large landmasses such as Australia or Africa

deciduous trees that lose their leaves in autumn

desert very dry area that receives very little rainfall

diprotodons large, four-legged, plant-eating animals

environments the land, water, air, and plants in particular areas

extinct no longer existing

forest places where many trees grow close together

frosts ice crystals that cover the ground and plants overnight

gases substances that consist of tiny particles that are spaced far apart

glaciers slow-moving rivers of ice, made from hardened snow

hemisphere half a sphere; for example, either the top (north) or bottom (south) half of Earth

ice sheets very thick sheets of ice on land

ice shelves thick ice that extends out from the ice sheet over the sea

mass extinctions when many of types of living things die out over a short period of time

meteorites rocks from space that have landed on Earth

microscopic describes something so small that it can only be seen with a microscope

migrated traveled from one place to another to live

monsoon wind that brings the summer rain to tropical areas; heavy seasonal rain

poles top and bottom of Earth

radiation energy from the Sun such as heat and light

rays beams of energy from the Sun such as heat and light

Sahara desert in north Africa; largest hot desert in the world

satellite humanmade spacecraft that orbits Earth

sea level height of the surface of the ocean

solar power electricity made from sunlight

vapor gas

vegetation type of plants that grow in an area

volcanoes mountains with an opening that sometimes releases burning hot gases and melted rock, or lava

windbreaks trees or structures that provide shelter from wind

Index